GOLF DIRTY TRICKS
An Unofficial BGA Guide

BAD BUT PROUD

BGA

BAD · ASSN.

GOLFERS

Illustrations copyright © 1994 by Barrie Maguire.

Golf Dirty Tricks is produced by becker&mayer, Ltd.

Typesetting by Dona MacAdam, Mac on the Hill

Cover illustration by Barrie Maguire

Becker, Jim.
   Golf dirty tricks: 50 ways to lie, cheat, and steal your way to victory by Jim Becker, Andy Mayer & Rick Wolff.
      p. cm.
ISBN: 0-8362-4224-6; $8.95
   1. Golf — Humor, 2. Golf–Corrupt practices. 3. Deception, I. Mayer, Andrew, 1954.   II. Wolff, Rick, 1951.   III. Title.
GV967.B445   1994
796,332'0207 — dc20   93-41142
                                                           CIP

99 00 01 BIN 10

Thanks to Matt Lombardi and Allan Stark

GOLF DIRTY TRICKS
50 Ways to Lie, Cheat, and Steal Your Way to Victory

by Jim Becker, Andy Mayer, & Rick Wolff
Illustrations by Barrie Maguire

Andrews and McMeel
A Universal Press Syndicate Company

Kansas City

Foreword

The Bad Golfers Association was established to serve, support, and inform the average golfer. The BGA defines the average golfer to be "someone whose love of the game exceeds his or her ability to play it." That pretty much describes every golfer in the universe. The BGA is not an association for hackers, it is an association for less gifted golfers. In other words, the BGA is not the PGA. BGA members are the ones who do not have Nick Faldo's repeating swing or Fred Couples's nerves of steel or Greg Norman's swagger or Ben Crenshaw's putting eye.

What BGA members offer the game is everlasting devotion. We have surrendered to a game that more often than not either seems to ignore our love or laughs at it. There is no doubt that golf is an addiction. However, help is here. The BGA is the first support group formed to help golfers cope with this all consuming sport. The BGA is your emotional safety net.

As is the USGA, the BGA is dedicated to the integrity and dignity of the game. There is no reason why a golfer can't shoot 98 and still be honest and courteous. Unless, of course, a player becomes totally crazed at the prospect of losing money to an undeserving opponent.

The BGA cannot and will not ever officially acknowledge the existence of dirty tricks in the game of golf. However, the membership does recognize the fact that some dirty tricks are more effective than others and, therefore, we unofficially (yet wholeheartedly) endorse this book. *Golf Dirty Tricks* is the bible for golfers who from time to time need an edge.

If you would like to join the BGA and receive a membership card, the rule book, and the quarterly BGA newsletter, send $9.95 to: BGA World Headquarters, c/o UniMedia, 4520 Main Street, Kansas City, MO 64111.

*This book is dedicated to golfers everywhere who strive
to lower their scores by any means possible.*

Teeing off

Flat-Top Tees

The key to winning at golf is *not* to improve your own game, but rather to destroy your opponent psychologically. That's where the *Flat-Top Tee* comes in.

After you tee off with a regular tee, remove one of these tees from your pocket and offer it to your opponent as the gentlemanly thing to do. When he is unable to get his golf ball to stay atop the tee, suggest that perhaps the breeze is blowing stronger than it seems to be—or maybe he's just nervous about playing against you.

Net gain: Adds minimum of one stroke to your opponent's score.

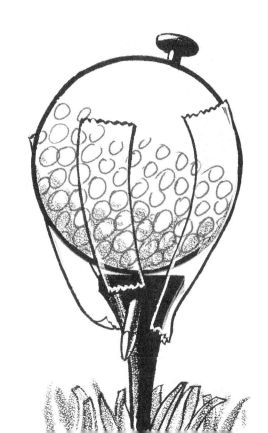

Eyeball Visualization

As you approach the tee box, make small talk with your opponent. Begin to tell him about the hideous car wreck you witnessed the other day. Give graphic details. Let your imagination go. As your opponent tees up his golf ball, wrap up your gory tale with this line: *"And one of their eyes had rolled right out of its socket! You know what it looked like? It looked just like a golf ball!"*

Now stand back, off to the side, and allow your opponent to concentrate on his drive.

Net gain: Adds one or more strokes to your opponent's score.

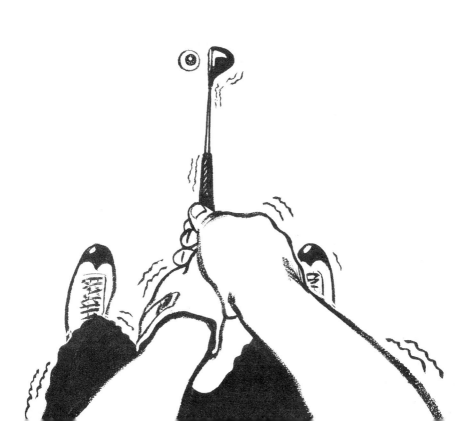

The Double Drive

While your opponent is getting ready for his tee shot, quickly distract him for a moment. Then, replace his ball with one of your own. Allow him to hit away.

Now it is your turn to tee off. Whichever of the two drives is better, that is the ball you will play next. If your opponent protests that you are playing his ball, simply point out that it is *you*, and not *he*, who is playing this brand of ball. When he is unable to find his ball, show a lot of sympathy and then kindly remind him that he must take an extra stroke for a lost ball.

Net gain: Adds 10–300+ yards to your drive plus one extra stroke to your opponent's score.

The Get a Good Grip Approach

When your opponent is looking the other way and admiring the scenery, apply a fine coating of Vaseline jelly to the handle of his driver.

Then, as he grips his club tightly and starts to tee off, be certain to stand *way off* to the side. *Way off.*

Net gain: Adds at least one stroke to your opponent's score plus infliction of heavy psychological damage.

The Ball Washer Ploy

Carry a small container of concentrated liquid soap with you on the course. When your opponent appears ready to clean his ball, discreetly empty the contents of your container into the ball washer.

Stand back and enjoy as your opponent's ball—and hands, and arms—become engulfed in soap bubbles. The more your opponent slips through the suds trying to retrieve his ball, the more bubbles he produces—and the soapier his ball becomes.

Net gain: Leaves your opponent's hands with a soapy film that just won't go away.

The Honor Code Ploy

Before teeing off on the first hole, do the gentlemanly thing: volunteer to keep score for both you and your opponent. If he protests, remind him gently that golf is a game based upon the honor code. Once your opponent is satisfied with your assurances of fair play, do, in fact, keep score. Just be certain to cheat—either inflate your opponent's scores or deflate your scores on a frequent basis throughout the match.

Net gain: Can either add 10–15 strokes to your opponent's score or subtract 10–15 strokes from your score.

The Sticky Tee Approach

If your opponent has been having a difficult time on the links and is still grousing about the *Flat-Top Tee* ploy, take pity on him: help him out by teeing up his next shot for him.

While placing the tee in the turf, add a couple of drops of Super Glue to the top of your opponent's tee. Then place his ball on top of the tee, stand back, and act innocent.

Then offer sympathy.

Net gain: Adds one extra stroke to your opponent's score, along with emotional stress.

The Ball Brand Ploy

Always give your opponent a very expensive ball to tee off with. After all, it's a well-known rule of the game that the more expensive the golf ball, the more likely your opponent is to shank it, slice it, or hook it deep into the woods.

Net gain: Adds one stroke to your opponent's score, and subtracts several dollars from your wallet.

The Right of First Refusal Tactic

Let's assume that you step up and tee off with a long but misdirected shot. Tell your opponent that as long as you openly call your tee shot to

be a lousy effort *while the ball is still in flight*, then you have the inalienable right to try your shot again without the fear of a penalty stroke. Feel free to repeat as often as necessary.

Note: Not to be confused with a mulligan (unless your opponent doesn't understand what a mulligan is).

Net gain: Takes many extraneous strokes off your score.

The Look Out for Flying Divots Strategy

While your opponent is getting ready for his tee shot, stand approximately 10 feet behind him. This is a good time to work in some practice swings with your wedge.

Be certain to scoop up some very large divots with your practice strokes. Watch them fly over your opponent's head as he tries to concentrate on his next drive. Your opponent will find this very distracting. Guaranteed.

Net gain: Should add at least one extra stroke to your opponent's score.

The Old Hole-in-One Trick

On a par-three hole, try to tee off when your opponent is distracted and looking the other way. If your shot's a good one, then play it.

However, if it's a poor shot—particularly if it's off in the woods—tell your opponent that you've made a *great* shot. Then, when you get to the green, have another ball hidden in your hand, bend down to the hole, and "remove" the ball from the cup. Exclaim to your opponent: "Why, I can't believe it! It's a hole in one!"

Net gain: Will remove at least two strokes and probably more from your score.

The Gracious Compliment Ploy

After each of your opponent's drives, yell "Fore!" at the top of your lungs, regardless of whether the ball is actually headed toward someone.

When your opponent begins to tire of this practice on every hole, explain to him that you're merely trying to warn the foursome that's ahead of you—especially in light of the fact that your esteemed opponent hits such lengthy drives.

Net gain: At some point your opponent will be distracted by this ploy and will flub at least one or two drives.

The Pacemaker Ploy

If you are behind as you begin play on the back nine, mention to your opponent in passing that you recently had a pacemaker implanted. No need to worry, though. As long as you can avoid undue stress (such as losing a friendly wager on the golf course...) the "old ticker" will be just fine. At least that's what your doctor said.

Net gain: Guarantees all mulligans and gimmes, except when playing against highly insensitive louts.

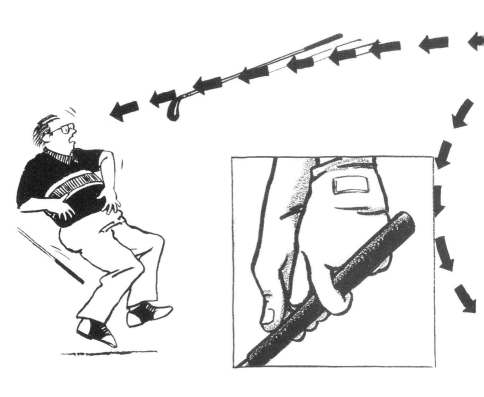

The Practice Swing Eliminator

If you find yourself down as you approach the final hole, you may have to physically remove your opponent from the competition.

A practice swing off the tee box can *accidentally* strike your opponent—if you know how and when to let go of your club. Such a blow can easily remove your opponent from active play, and he will be forced to default the match to you.

Consult the accompanying diagram for the proper club grip for *The Practice Swing Eliminator*.

Net gain: Total opponent default.

The Kill 'em with Kindness Ploy

Heap tons of praise on your opponent *right before* he makes his shot. That way he's going to try to live up to your expectations. And everyone knows what happens when you try to do that—you fail! Here's what you say:

On the tee: "They tell me you have one of the most natural power swings in the game. I can't wait to see you tee off..."

On the green: "Most amateur golfers, like myself, always freeze up before a big putt. But for a top player like you, this putt is going to be sooo easy..."

Remember to register your disbelief after he misses that putt that was "sooo easy."

Net gain: Your opponent will thank you and then shank one, badly.

Fairways

Out of the Rough and off the Cuff

This is a tried-and-true winner: Wear loose-fitting but fashionable trousers with big, big cuffs. Before play begins, stash an extra ball in each cuff.

If one of your approach shots heads into the rough, move to the edge of the fairway where your ball has exited play. As you look for your ball, gently lift an extra ball out of your cuff, using your wedge as a scoop. Lucky you—there's your "lost" ball! And you thought it had gone into the rough!

Replace extra cuff balls as needed.

Net gain: Saves one or two strokes from your score.

The Serpentine Strategy

Remind your opponent that one needs strong nerves to play golf.

Then plant a rubber snake in his golf bag next to his putter.

Net Gain: Your opponent will become flustered, upset, and anxious.

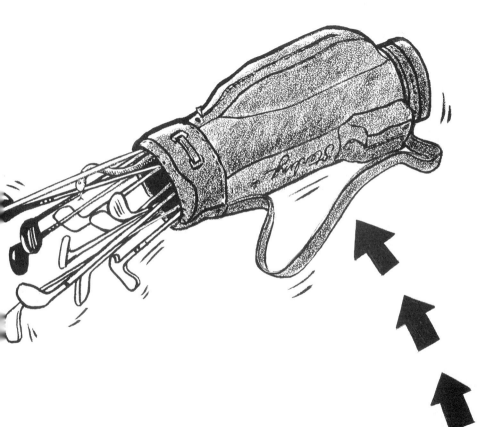

The Sudden Death Strategy

If your opponent is trusting and a bit naïve, take the opportunity to instruct him where to stand during an electrical storm.

Tell him that the safest strategy is to run to the middle of the fairway, take his one-iron, and point out from what direction the last bolt of lightning came.

Net gain: Your opponent defaults match, life.

The Doggy Doo-Doo Dodge

Walk ahead to where your opponent's drive has landed. Crouch over the ball, and then carefully place a wad of fake dog doody right behind your opponent's ball.

Remind your opponent that golf regulations stipulate that the ball shall

be played as it lies, except as otherwise provided for in the rules. Unfortunately, there's nothing about doggy doo-doo in the rules. (Note: Fake doggy doo-doo is available in most novelty stores. In a pinch, though, feel free to use the real thing. It has the same effect.)

Net gain: Your opponent will have to play a new ball (one penalty stroke). Suggest that he use ball washer on next hole (see *Dirty Trick #5*).

The Schwarzenegger Strategy

Before your opponent heads out on the course, throw about 60 to 70 extra old balls into his bag. Make certain that they are hidden well below his clubs, out of sight.

Watch the fun as your opponent lugs his golf bag around all day. Add to the humor by commenting on how much he seems to be struggling with his bag and how much he's perspiring.

Net gain: Should add several strokes to your opponent's score—or perhaps, on a very hot day, a real stroke.

The Accidental Gearshift Ploy

An overconfident golfer with a low handicap must not be allowed to find his rhythm. Here's a way to keep him guessing.

As he climbs behind the wheel of the golf cart and starts to brag about his play, quietly slip the cart into reverse. Hold on tightly when your opponent hits the accelerator, only to find himself (and you) heading backward.

For greater fun, make sure the golf cart is parked only a few feet in front of a water hazard. Place in reverse, hold on, and hold your breath.

Net gain: Your opponent loses deposit on golf cart.

The Canadian Goose Honk, Eh? Ruse

While you're out on the course, show off your brand-new goose call, which is guaranteed to lure every Canadian goose within 10 miles to your spot. Feel free to blow the goose call throughout the match.

Make certain to bring along a pair of heavy-duty boots. Put them on when the geese begin to show up.

Net gain: Will add two or three strokes to your opponent's score and ruin his shoes.

The Thieving Animal Dodge

Explain to your opponent that the reason why you can't find your ball is that it's been stolen by an animal. (Likely culprits include squirrels, raccoons, chipmunks, gophers, etc.) This is only to be expected, particularly when one of your shots lands in a trap or in rough terrain.

Because there's no accounting for the random acts of burglary by God's little creatures, you can simply replace your ball and play on.

Net gain: No penalty stroke added to your score.

The Ground Under Repair Ruse

Be certain to carry a can of white spray paint in your golf bag for those shots that end up in a bad lie. On the sly, simply spray a white circle around your ball, claim it to be "ground under repair," and take a free drop onto a preferable spot.

Explain to your opponent that this is all quite legitimate under the rules of play.

Net gain: Will save you as many strokes as you have spray paint.

The Fear of Lyme Disease Fakery

If your ball strays into rough terrain or shrubbery *that gives every indication that it might contain ticks*, then disregard that shot, pull out another ball, and try again.

Explain to your opponent that several golfers have contracted Lyme disease while searching for errant shots. Point out that course rules dictate that there's no reason to risk your health by chasing a ball into the rough. Since your health is more important than a silly golf ball, no penalty stroke is given.

Net gain: Subtracts at least one stroke from your score.

The Leave 'em in the Trail Trick

When loading golf bags onto the cart, accidentally forget to secure the safety strap that holds your opponent's bag in place.

Sooner or later the bag will fall off, strewing your opponent's clubs across the cart path.

Net gain: Your opponent will be concerned about the condition of his clubs for the rest of the round.

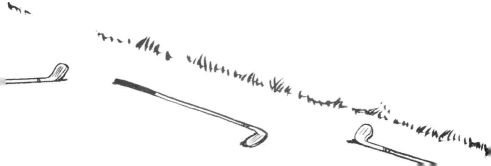

The Itchy Trigger Finger Trap

While you are at your local novelty shop buying some fake doggy-doody (see *Dirty Trick #19*), also purchase a can of itching powder.

Sprinkle said powder into your opponent's golf glove before you start play.

> **Net gain: Your opponent may have to default if he can't hold a golf club.**

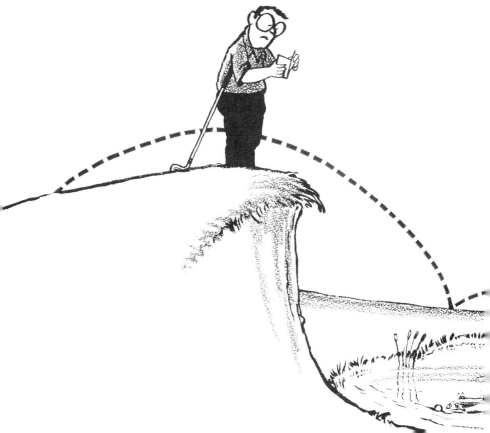

DIRTY TRICK #28

The Bogus Map Ploy

If your opponent is new to the course and isn't sure how a particular hole is to be played, have a fake or misleading course map on hand. Be more than eager to help out your opponent by showing him the way on the map.

Prepare to be most apologetic after your opponent's drive splashes into that hidden water hazard that wasn't indicated on the "outdated" map.

Net gain: Adds at least one stroke to your opponent's score.

The Sociable Host Approach

Pack identical flasks in your golf bag—one filled with water, the other with scotch. After taking several conspicuous swigs of the water, do the old switcheroo and offer your opponent a shot of the hard stuff from the other flask.

Repeat throughout the round until respective flasks are empty.

Net gain: Should add a solid 10 strokes to your opponent's score.

Greens

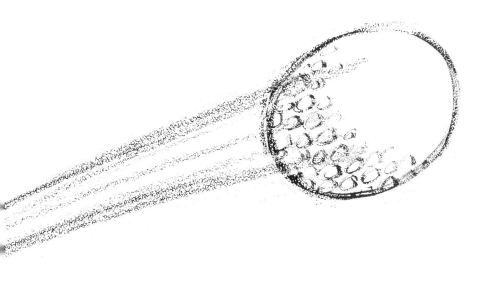

The Six-Foot Gimme

When your ball comes to rest anywhere within six feet of the cup, this is a gimme. Never ask permission from your opponent. Simply remove the ball before he can protest, and add one stroke to your final score for this hole. If he *does* protest, tell him that he should have said something *before* you picked your ball up.

When your *opponent's* ball is close to the cup, point out to him that there is nothing in the PGA rules about "gimmes." Insist that he hole all of his putts.

Net gain: Will definitely save one or two strokes from your score.

The Flag Pull and Plant Ploy

On a long putt, offer to tend the flag for your opponent. When he's not looking, remove the flagstick and drive it firmly into the green several inches from the actual cup.

Now move your foot to fully cover the location of the actual cup. Remember to look alert and smile.

Net gain: Adds one stroke to your opponent's score.

The Flying Bird Shadow-Puppet Show

When your opponent is ready to putt, position yourself facing the hole with the sun to your back. The instant before his putter strikes the ball, make a *Flying Bird Shadow Puppet*. (Please refer to our illustration.)

To be fully effective, your bird must fly for only a second or two—treading that fine line between, *"Is that a real bird?"* and *"Are you trying to mess with my head?"*

Net gain: Adds one stroke to your opponent's score and messes with his head.

The British Bump

If you are faced with a difficult putt, but your opponent's ball is within easy striking range, don't line up your shot with the cup but rather with your opponent's ball. Use your putter and take a full swing—striking your opponent's ball off the green.

If your opponent protests such a shot and claims that he can put his ball back in its original position, explain that you are playing by old standard British rules, according to which the "croquet approach shot" is perfectly acceptable.

> **Net gain: Adds one to three strokes to your opponent's score.**

Reflecting on Your Opponent's Game

Just as your opponent is ready to hit that critical putt, take out a pair of mirrored sunglasses, pretend to clean them, and "accidentally" shine the sun's glare into his eyes.

Apologize to your opponent, but also remind him that there's no such thing as "do-overs" when putting.

Net gain: Adds one or two strokes to your opponent's game.

The Law of Gravity Gaffe

If your well-struck putt happens to pass over an open cup and inexplicably doesn't fall in, simply pick your ball up and count the putt as being in the hole.

Explain to your opponent that the law of gravity always supersedes the laws of golf, and under such law, your ball *should* have gone in the cup. Why it didn't you can't explain. But certainly that's no reason why you should be penalized.

Net gain: Subtracts one or two strokes from your score.

The D-Cell Marker

When it comes to marking your ball on the green, try to be creative.

Instead of using a dime, penny, or some other small, flat, insignificant marker, carry along a D-size battery in your bag. Use the battery to mark your ball; you'll find that it will not blow away in the breeze and that it will definitely get in the way of your opponent's shot.

If, for some reason, your opponent protests, remove your battery before he putts—leaving behind a craterlike indentation.

Net gain: Adds one stroke to your opponent's score.

The On-the-Level Ploy

Carry a carpenter's level in your golf bag to test the roll of the green when putting.

Then take the level, lay it on its side, and push it down into the green so as to make a nice little trench that will lead your ball directly to the cup.

If your opponent protests, ask him to show you precisely where in the PGA rule book it says that carpenter's levels are illegal.

Net gain: Will save you countless putting strokes.

The Electronic Pager Ploy

Be sure to carry your electronic pager at all times on the course. Keep it on your belt or in your pocket.

"Test" your beeper just when your opponent is ready to putt. Remark to your opponent: "Yes—isn't it just an amazing coincidence that my beeper goes off just as you're trying to putt out?"

Offer sympathy.

Net gain: Will add numerous strokes to your opponent's putting game.

The Halitosis Knock-Out Punch

Keep a raw onion in your golf bag. Take several big bites during the course of play. Enjoy.

Then lean close to your opponent and offer him plenty of "up-close-and-personal" golfing advice as he lines up his next crucial putt.

Net gain: Serious damage to your opponent's nose.

The Pre-Recorder Scorecard Ruse

Take the time to fully fill out a scorecard *before* you start play. Attempt to predict as accurately as possible what you think you and your opponent will shoot for the day. Then shave at least one stroke off each of *your* holes.

Keep the scorecard in your pocket, and be ready to produce it as you and your opponent march off to the 19th hole.

Be certain to dispose properly and discreetly of the real scorecard.

Net gain: Will probably eliminate 10–15 shots off your score.

Traps

The Sand Trap Trap

When an approach shot by your opponent lands in a sand trap, find his ball before he does. Then step firmly on the ball with the toe of your shoe and bury the ball deep into the sand so that it's well hidden.

When your opponent cannot find his ball, suggest it might be in another bunker. Don't forget to remind him that he must add a stroke for a lost ball.

Net gain: Adds several strokes to your opponent's score, plus immense frustration.

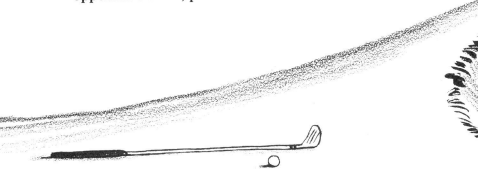

The Hand Mashie Maneuver

When faced with a difficult trap shot, employ the *hand mashie* approach. Simply pick your ball up—when your opponent is looking the other way—and toss it onto the green.

For best effect, be sure to throw a little sand onto the green along with your ball.

Net gain: Cuts one or two shots off your score.

The Drop Shot Shot

On occasion, you will have to resort to a drop ball. Play by the rules.

Simply extend your arm horizontally and drop the ball, but be careful that the ball "accidentally" hits your toe and that you "accidentally" kick the ball to where you want it to be.

Net gain: Saves one or two strokes off your score.

The First Rule of Golf

When struggling in a sand trap or any other hazard, always remember this: *It ain't a stroke if nobody else saw it.*

Be certain to employ this philosophy throughout your golfing career.

Net gain: Saves you countless strokes.

Dirty Trick #45

The Rakish Approach

When your opponent is playing a shot near a bunker, remove the bunker rake when he's not looking and place it directly behind him with the rake's prongs pointing up.

After your opponent makes his shot and turns around, there's a 50-50 chance that he'll step on the rake and smack himself in the face.

Net gain: Always used to work for the Three Stooges.

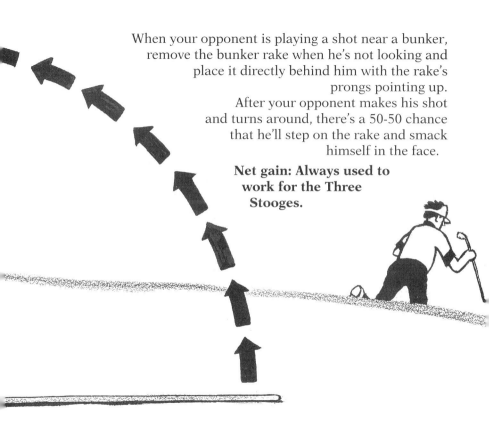

Clubhouse

The Color-Blind Test

Embarrass your opponent. Emerge from the clubhouse wearing bright plaid knickers, bright yellow socks, and a purple-and-orange shirt with large polka dots.

If your opponent protests your sartorial splendor, tell him that this is your "lucky" apparel.

Be sure to wave to all the other golfers as you make your way around the course.

Net gain: Possible opponent default if your clothes are *really* ugly.

The Fiery Car Trick

Become friends with the attendant in the clubhouse. Slip him a few bills, give the attendant your opponent's license plate number, and tell him to announce over the course loudspeaker that your opponent's car is on fire.

Offer sympathy as your opponent races back to the parking lot.

Net gain: Probable default by your opponent due to anxiety attack.

The Forgotten Clubs Strategy

Offer to drive your opponent to the golf course. When you pick him up, make sure he's safely inside the car, buckling his seat belt,

before loading his clubs into your trunk.

Then, quietly remove the putter and nine-iron from his bag. Leave them both on his front lawn.

Drive away.

Net gain: Adds at least 10 strokes to your opponent's score.

The Dramamine Dodge

On the way to a new golf course, ask your opponent to serve as your copilot and to read the map and directions to get there.

Drive all over the road, hit every bump, and ride over every pothole until your opponent is good and queasy.

Net gain: Nausea should overcome your opponent and considerably weaken his game.

The Thinking Man's Guide to Golf

If you can make your opponent think and play at the same time, then you're well on your way to a winning round of golf. Here's what you say:

On the tee: "I read somewhere that the best drivers in the game always exhale right when they're in midswing. Do you?"

On the green: "Have you ever noticed how you tend to squeeze your club awfully tightly when you putt out?"

That's all there is to it. Your opponent will take care of the rest.

> **Net gain: Your opponent will think his way into several double bogeys.**

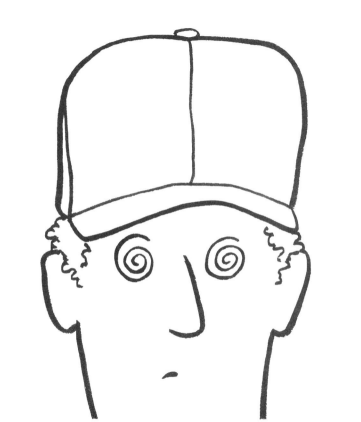

About the Authors

Jim Becker is an avid tennis player, bowler, football, baseball, and basketball player. He has never played golf.

Andy Mayer lowered his handicap by 20 strokes by following each and every one of the dirty tricks outlined in this book. With a handicap now of just under 100, he is able to complete a full round of golf in six hours flat.

Rick Wolff was disqualified for life from the PGA during the 1990 U.S. Open for using Dirty Trick #16. In so doing, Rick proved the importance of executing all tricks in this book with "the greatest of care."

Barrie Maguire bears a striking resemblance to the guy pictured cheating throughout this book. (At least, when he had hair he did.)